BY THE SAME AUTHOR

Poetry

Looking for Peace

A Soldier's Time

Deeply Dug In

No Turning Back: The Battle of Dien Bien Phu

As Editor

The Selected Poems of Yvor Winters

The Selected Letters of Yvor Winters

The Selected Poems of Janet Lewis

LEARNING WAR

LEARNING WAR
SELECTED VIETNAM WAR POEMS

R.L. BARTH

Greenwich Exchange
London

Acknowledgments

These poems are drawn from the following collections: *Battlefield Prayer* (Scienter Press, 2003); *Deeply Dug In* (University of New Mexico Press, 2003); *Looking for Peace* (Abattoir Editions, 1985); *No Turning Back* (Scienter Press, 2016); *A Soldier's Time* (John Daniel, 1987); and the broadside *War and Peace* (Scienter Press, 2005). Some of these poems have been revised.

Greenwich Exchange, London

First published in Great Britain in 2021
All rights reserved

Learning War: Selected Vietnam War Poems
© R.L. Barth, 2021

This book is sold subject to the conditions that it shall not, by way of trade or otherwise, be lent, resold, hired out or otherwise circulated without the publisher's prior consent in any form of binding or cover other than that in which it is published and without a similar condition including this condition being imposed on the subsequent purchaser.

Printed and bound by imprintdigital.com
Cover design by December Publications
Tel: 07951511275

Greenwich Exchange website: www.greenex.co.uk

Cataloguing in Publication Data
is available from the British Library

Cover art courtesy of Shutterstock

ISBN: 978-1-910996-56-0

To Susan, Ann and Eric

Wherfore my worde is still (I change it not)
That *Warre seems sweete to such as raunge it not.*
                                    – George Gascoigne

CONTENTS

Introduction/15

Reading the *Iliad* / 21

I. DEEPLY DUG IN

'Go tell the Spartans ... ' / 23

Battlefield Prayer / 23

Saigon: 16 vi. 1963 / 25

War Debt / 25

Allegory for L.B.J. / 25

Under Fire / 26

Initial Confusion / 26

Indoctrination / 26

Bush Discipline / 27

A Child Accidentally Napalmed / 27

Terminology / 27

One Way to Carry the Dead / 28

An Old Story / 28

War Story; or, How Hard Was It? / 28

Xin Loi / 29

Movie Stars / 29

For Unused Graves / 29

Saigon: 30 iv. 1975 / 30

Epitaph / 30

Up Against the Wall / 30

Epilogue / 31

II. LOOKING FOR PEACE

Letter from a Staging Area / 35

A Letter to the Dead / 37

A Letter from an Observation Post: Near An Hoa / 38

Nightpiece / 39

The Insert / 40

The Patrol / 41

Swift, Silent, Deadly / 42

A Letter to My Infant Son / 43

A Letter from the Bush / 45

Outpost Overrun / 46

A Letter from An Hoc (4), by a Seedbed / 47

Letter from a Ward / 49

Chaplain to Bishop / 50

POWs / 51

Da Nang Nights / 52

Running in Vietnam / 53

Office of the Dead / 54

Sniper / 55

First Watch / 56

Short-Timer: Six and a Wakeup / 57

Souvenirs / 58

Elegy for a Dead Friend / 59

'The Lighter That Never Fails' / 60

Last Letter / 61

Meditations after Battle / 62

Fieldcraft / 63

A Letter from the World / 64

III. SMALL ARMS FIRE

'Why not adjust? Forget this? ... ' / 65

De Bello / 65

'Patrolling silently ... ' / 67

Definition / 67

SOP / 67

Social Darwinism / 68

For Part of a Generation / 68

'Don't you know your poems are hurtful?' / 68

Grunt Fantasy / 69

Epitaph for the Fallen at Camerone / 69

Foxhole Theology / 69

Martial 8.58 / 70

Reading the Op-Ed Page / 70

Incoming! / 70

As Good as It Gets / 71

'Tonight you bitch ... ' / 71

After the War / 71

Lessons of War / 72

'Kentucky's Money Bonus' / 72

Ambush / 72

MIAs / 73

A Little Elegy for Jimmy Stewart / 73

Snapshot, RVN / 73

'I swore I'd only be ... ' / 74

Epitaph for a Patrol Leader / 74

IV. CODA

Republic of Vietnam Campaign Medal with Device / 77

Introduction

Taking a close look at one of the poems in this volume seems to me a useful way to introduce all of them. Here is 'Xin Loi' in its entirety:

> A sucking chest wound's nature's way
> Of saying, 'Jack, this ain't your day.'

This poem is almost as brief as a poem in English can be – a single rhyming couplet, two lines of iambic tetrameter, sixteen syllables, more brief than a haiku. It is an epigram and places its author, R.L. Barth, in a tradition that stretches back to *The Greek Anthology* and comes forward through the works of the Roman poet Martial, a poet Barth has translated (his version of a Martial epigram is included in this volume), and the Elizabethan epigrammatists, to the relatively recent American poet J.V. Cunningham. Cunningham is associated with Yvor Winters, the poet and critic, a writer Barth acknowledges as an influence and the man who more than any other identified, described, and urged the virtues of the tradition to which Barth belongs, the tradition of the Plain or Native style. Barth has edited a selection of Winters's poems and a collection of his letters, no doubt using scholarship as a way of paying tribute. An awareness of this tradition can help us understand the kind of poems Barth writes.

One of the purposes of poems in this tradition is to provide definitions. The little poem we are considering in fact takes the form of a definition of 'a sucking chest wound' – not a technical, medical definition, but an imaginative one. This imaginative definition uses onomatopoeia in its first line, 'A sucking chest wound's nature's way' – the repetitive, rhythmic s-sounds serve to imitate the chilling noises made by the type of wound being defined. This practice continues in the beginning of the next line, 'Of saying' – yet another s-sound and one tied to a word that, through parallelism, presents a transformation from 'sucking' to 'saying', from making noises to making sense. This transformation justifies the bit of dialogue that concludes the second line and the poem, 'Jack, this ain't your day', suggesting that nature's language and point-of-view are similar to those of Dirty Harry, a point-of-view that is at once both grimly comic and somehow sympathetic.

Nature, an abstraction, is incapable of saying anything, so the definition uses personification to permit nature to speak, thus raising the question of the identity of the speaker of the poem. This little poem appears to be not only an imaginative definition but also a tiny dramatic monologue.

While the speaker of the poem is ultimately its author, we notice the absence of the first person singular from it, causing us to consider at least the possibility that it might be spoken by someone else – possibly the person suffering from the wound or, more likely, a witness to someone suffering from it. The objectivity of the poem suggests that the speaker's point-of-view is retrospective, and the speaker is therefore someone who has been haunted by the sounds and sights of such a wound and finally feels compelled to write about it as a way of establishing distance from the memory. I would say it is not necessary to have once confronted an actual sucking chest wound to be haunted in this way – seeing and hearing one in a training film or even being exposed to a vivid verbal description of one would be quite enough to fix it in the memory.

A little dramatic monologue requires a setting. The wound that is the trigger for this poem could have happened in France in 1945 or in 1915, or yesterday in Afghanistan, or today in Yemen.

I suppose such a wound might have occurred when an arrow

was pulled from a chest at Agincourt or when a sword pierced a chest before the walls of Troy. Barth makes this historic sense explicit in a number of his poems. 'Reading the *Iliad*', for instance, calls on the reader to compare a veteran's recent memories with the feats performed by Homer's heroes, and 'A Letter to the Dead', addressed to three English poets of the First World War – Wilfred Owen, Edmund Blunden, and Siegfried Sassoon – concludes, 'War's war. We are, my friends, no different.' Barth establishes the scene of his brief dramatic monologue with its title, 'Xin Loi'.

For some readers, this title could merely consist of strange, unpronounceable words – perhaps a rough equivalent of the apparently meaningless sounds made by a sucking chest wound. Other readers would at least recognize the language of the title as Vietnamese. Readers for whom the title would mean the most are those who recognize it as a phrase pronounced by Americans in Vietnam as 'sin loy' and translated by them as 'Sorry about that', a phrase with a multitude of applications ranging from a sardonic response to news of an accidental bombing of civilians to a joking apology for an ill-timed fart. Nature's message to the dying trooper in this poem – I do not think it is too far-fetched to suggest that the final s-sound in the word 'this' represents the final sound made by the wound as its victim dies – is a kind of translation and expansion of the poem's title, a kind of overt tough mindedness that protects a tenderness that might otherwise be overwhelmed by pity.

Combat troops have no monopoly on sucking chest wounds or other causes of death. We live in a time of all but constant wars in which civilians are often primary targets and the current pandemic has made exceedingly clear just how widespread death can be in a time of relative peace. Even if weddings and births are as important, if not more important, than funerals in our lives, the human condition is dominated by death. War, combat, heightens the awareness of this element of the human condition, threatening that condition with a sense of meaninglessness. Poems are the result of a compulsion to make sense – sense of the kind that can squeeze the heart and catch the throat – of what might otherwise seem meaningless. The concentration and passion required to achieve this result is the reason Barth's two lines incorporate without being at all weighed down by so much craft, technique – meter, rhyme, an internal rhyme, onomatopoeia, personification, dialogue, and so on. In the same way, the poems in this volume display a wide range of forms and techniques – epigrams, rhymed quatrains, sonnets, blank verse, syllabics, verse epistles – without being at all literary in a negative way. Barth's technique is always in the service of his meaning and of what for lack of a better word must be called his inspiration.

For me, R.L. Barth's Vietnam war poems are first and foremost poems. I have written at such length about such a brief poem because the ability to do so profitably provides evidence that it *is* a poem, a collection of words that cannot only bear, but will repay, numerous rereadings. Poems are rare in any age and are especially rare in our time. The only appropriate response to the rewards and pleasures poems offer is gratitude. I am grateful for these poems, and I think it likely you will be too.

– Warren Hope

Reading the *Iliad*

Volume and desk, coffee and cigarette
Forgotten, the reader, held in Homer's mind,
Looks upon Greeks and Trojans fighting yet,
The heroes and foot-soldiers, thin and blind,

Forced-marching for the Styx. But suddenly
Stunned by the clamor under smoky skies,
Boasting and taunting, he looks up to see –
Not the god-harried plain where Hector tries

His destiny, not the room; instead, a mountain
Covered with jungle; on one slope, a chateau
With garden, courtyard, a rococo fountain,
And, faces down, hands tied, six bodies in a row.

I

Deeply Dug In

'Go tell the Spartans ... '

Go tell the Spartans that we hold this land,
Deeply dug in, obeying their command.

Battlefield Prayer

The dead a-gibbering, and we who ken
Hear 'Fuck it! Don't mean nothin'.' Yeah. Amen.

Saigon: 16 vi. 1963

In chaos, judgment took on form and name:
The lotus flared; men burned in your just flame.

War Debt

Survive or die, war holds one truth:
Marine, you will not have a youth.

Allegory for L.B.J.

So many Isaacs, Abraham!
You needn't even lash
Poor boys to altars; seek no ram;
Just raise your knife and slash.

Under Fire

How many, Captain Dawkins, did you send,
Without crowds cheering, to a lonesome end?

Initial Confusion

A sergeant barked, 'Your ass is Uncle's!' though
It wasn't clear if he meant Sam or Ho.

Indoctrination

'First, know the jungle and your enemy;
Learn fieldcraft; use bush discipline; keep this
Firmly in mind: we've kinds of syphilis
Without known treatment – that is, have no truck
With cyclo-girls; and then I'll guarantee
That you'll survive your thirteen months. With luck.'

Bush Discipline

Rigged branch. Chubb lost a hand. With Charlie near
None celebrate till safely in the rear.

A Child Accidentally Napalmed

'Why waste your tears on me? Give over grief.
If I knew horror, yet my life was brief.'
Some mourner will perhaps say that for me.
I'd say, 'I suffered an eternity.'

Terminology

He humps the mountains in monsoon and mist
Who has no woman, is no pantheist.

One Way to Carry the Dead

A huge shell thundered; he was vaporized
And, close friends breathing near, internalized.

An Old Story

'Hustle the boom-boom girls up here,
But take precautions, hey? I've sent
Back for the rum. We'll drink down fear.
Why should our watch be different?'

War Story; or, How Hard Was It?

Monk mumbled the Psalms, even pulling guard,
Until they fragged his ass. It was that hard.

Xin Loi

A sucking chest wound's nature's way
Of saying, 'Jack, this ain't your day.'

Movie Stars

Bob Hope, John Wayne, and Martha Raye
Were dupes who knew no other way;
Jane Fonda, too, whose Hanoi hitch
Epitomized protester kitsch.

For Unused Graves

These never died but – was it self-deceit? –
Warred, armed with placards, down an unmined street.

Saigon: 30 iv. 1975

We lie here, trampled in the rout;
There was no razor's edge, no doubt.

Epitaph

Tell them quite simply that we died
Thirsty, betrayed, and terrified.

Up Against the Wall

These dead troops gave their country fame,
Which country travestied their story.
Now, only kin recall each name;
Only the dead recall their glory.

Epilogue

Twenty years later, the poor sons of bitches
Learn jungle rot, decaying flesh, still itches
And, spreading body part by body part,
Even corrupts the chambers of the heart.

II

Looking for Peace

We looked for peace, but no good came,
for a time of healing, but behold, terror.
– Jeremiah 8:15

Letter from a Staging Area
arriving in-country, February 1968

1
I could see nothing beyond the window pane
But darkness – not a light on the wing tip
To trick the blackness and assume a context;
And yet, the crew chief stood, signaling us
To fasten seat belts and extinguish smokes.
We dropped. The plane soon touched down in Da Nang,
And I prepared to head for Indian Country,
As they say over here.

     A convoy waited
In a kind of alley formed by Quonset huts
And barbed-wire fencing. Sleepy drivers stood
In quiet groups, pulling on cigarettes
Held in cupped hands like small, erratic lanterns,
Or napped on front seats, while across the runways,
A line of Phantoms sortied into darkness.
The only other sounds were the rasped orders
Of officers who hustled us to trucks,
And our own clumsy scuffling, grabbing gear
And climbing over tail gates into truck beds.

The six-bys started up and then moved slowly
Through cratered streets. Vietnam had receded,
It seemed, to a mere feeling of thick dust
And smell of strange foods and decay (and fear
Through all the putrid stench). I could see little:
Only the darkness and, immediately
Behind our truck, two white slits, black-out lights.

2
Within a short time after our arrival,
The VC rocketed the staging area.
There's something terrifying – even more,
Something unreal in the incoming rounds.
I'd known of them, of course; and naturally
I'd feared them in an abstract sort of way.
(All the test firings in the States, on ranges
Set up much less to teach proficiency,
I think, than fear, were useless. And why not?
For it's one thing to marvel at the power,
The pure destructive force, you can inflict
On enemies; something else altogether
Imagining yourself those enemies.
It's just not possible.)

                        But there I was:
Asleep one minute, stumbling to war the next.
Suspended in impacted time,
I waited, hearing all too sharply
The thump and crash, the pings as smaller pieces
Of shrapnel hit tin bulkheads. What was it like?
Like suddenly the true Platonic forms
Shredded the shadows?

                        But I can't explain,
Not really. All I know is that I lay
In dark green skivvies, helmet, and flak-jacket,
Rooting, nose furrowing the trench's dust
(Closer to nature than I'd ever been),
Too stark in the pus-yellow light from flares;
Listening for exploding rocket rounds,
Yet hearing, too, the interrupting screams
And cursing wounded crying out for corpsmen,
And thinking, 'Okay, thirteen months to go.'

A Letter to the Dead

The outpost trench is deep with mud tonight.
Cold with the mountain winds and two weeks' rain,
I watch the concertina. The starlight-
Scope hums, and rats assault the bunkers again.

You watch with me: Owen, Blunden, Sassoon.
Through sentry duty, everything you meant
Thickens to fear of nights without a moon.
War's war. We are, my friends, no different.

A Letter from an Observation Post: Near An Hoa

Seeming to race the shadow line, eight men
Humped through the thigh-deep paddies – only Hodge
Moving with sureness, shoot by shoot, on point –
Until they neared a tree line. There, he knew,
Hidden within were ruins of a few hooches
Marked as a ville on maps, though long abandoned
By farmers, and by Charlie, during day.

As Hodge was turning to his newest men –
Dragging with six days' hacking mountainsides –
Mortars began to crump, sending them diving
Into the water behind the paddy dikes.
Small-arms fire snapped on both sides, bullets tearing
Through jungle and through mud.

                                        Detached by distance
From the fire fight, we watched it like small children
Who have not yet deadened imaginations,
As the shadow line swept village, ridge, and outpost.
Later that night, hearing the sound of choppers,
We saw, gathering darkness to its center,
Their red star cluster die above the trees.

Nightpiece

No moon, no stars, only the leech-black sky,
Until Puff rends the darkness, spewing out
His thin red flames, and then the quick reply
Of blue-green tracers climbing all about.
At night, such lovely ways to kill, to die.

The Insert

Our view of sky, jungle, and fields constricts
Into a sinkhole covered with saw-grass

Undulating, soon whipped slant as the chopper
Hovers at four feet. Rapt, boot-deep in slime,

We deploy ourselves in a loose perimeter,
Listening for incoming rockets above

The thump of rotor blades, edgy for contact,
Junkies of terror impatient to shoot up.

Nothing moves, nothing sounds; then, single file,
We move across a streambed toward high ground.

The terror of the insert's quickly over.
Too quickly ... and more quickly every time ...

The Patrol

We slipped through NVA patrols around
Supplies dug into mountains and a class
Outside a Quonset hut, where cadres scribbled
Tactics on a blackboard, all this beneath
The triple canopy deep in the mountains.

At times patrols passed barely three feet off,
While we knelt motionless and camouflaged.
I wanted a surprise assault right there,
But that was not our mission: ours to watch,
Call in intelligence and then *di-di*

As quietly as possible; and yet,
As we withdrew, someone stepped on a twig.
Time stopped ... The NVA began to gabble
And beat the bush, and I got on the horn
To call in air support to cover us.

As the two Phantoms dropped five hundred pounders,
The shrapnel spinning near and secondary
Explosions rocking the landscape, we moved
Through the thick undergrowth until, at last,
Emerging from the jungle, we set up

On a bare hilltop where we could observe
NVA sallies from the jungle, and
Laid out our fields of fire while radioing
For an emergency extraction *mau len*.
No choppers flew that evening. We dug in ...

Swift, Silent, Deadly
motto of the 1st Reconnaissance Bn., USMC

Somewhere, along the tangled mountain slopes,
Slyly edging the camps and villages,
The tiger pads.
                He is at once our emblem
And fear and, did he know, almost extinct.

A Letter to My Infant Son
outside Da Nang

Some day, when you are hunting attic trunks
Or hear your buddies boasting of brave fathers,
I know that, all excited, you will ask me
To tell war stories. How shall I answer you?

      I still remember my best childhood friends,
Two brothers. How I envied them! Their father
Had given them his medals and his chevrons,
And I remember fumbling with delight
The green and khaki stripes, the tarnished brass.
Happier, sitting still, I heard them tell
Their father's stories, which each night I worked
Through closely, casting and recasting them
In varied forms. Always, I was the hero.

      And so, my dear, how shall I answer you?
Shall I be silent when you ask – preferring
Childish amazement, even childish anger,
Trusting you to return with a child's kiss
And quick forgiveness?

                      War is not the story
That you would have me tell you, as I heard it.
And what is courage? Too many things, it seems:
Carelessness, fatalism, or an impulse.
Yet it is none of these. True courage is
Hidden in unexpected terms and places:
In performing simple duties day by day;
In sometimes saying 'no' when necessary;
In, most of all, refusing to despair.
Even suppose a man is brave one time –

Is truly brave, I mean – will he be brave
A second time? In other ways? Perhaps.

    There are few glorious stories in this war.
Small child, you will not comprehend the rot,
Disease, mud, rain; the mangled friend who curses
The chance that saved him (while you look at him,
Wishing him dead, almost); the bitterness
You realize you may not understand;
The children's bodies, small as yours is now ...
War is too much of sentimentality,
Which you soon learn is almost always brutal,
However sad, however pitiful.
So, when you ask some day to hear war stories,
Though I would have you truly understand,
How shall I answer you, if not with silence?

A Letter from the Bush

The triple canopy –
Huge trees, bamboo, and vines –
Constricting sight, we see
All day the jungle's designs
Close up: the next vine, leaf,
Branch, or arc of light
Erratic as our grief.
Engrossed, we never sight
Objects that, distant enough,
Permit an azimuth reading.

Nights, we set in – or bluff
The jungle when, proceeding
Noiselessly, each man paces
Himself, fixed on bright wood.
We learn decay that traces
Trails, clearings, even faces
In ambush. It is good.

Outpost Overrun

It was our sixth night. After throwing dice
To set the order of the watch, we slept.
During my watch, the listening post team slipped
Down the ridge. They only called in twice.

There was no other sound but the faint hum
Of radio handset just inside the bunker.
Across the valley, like a signal blinker,
A fire went out. Nothing but tedium ...

Next thing I knew, they were inside the wire:
The sappers first, and then a full platoon
Overran posts nobody could maintain.
We shot up flares and opened aimless fire

At everything that moved, trying to fight.
Wounded, I rolled into the garbage dump.
All I remember's my chest turning damp
And someone crying out, 'More light! More light!'

A Letter from An Hoc (4), by a Seedbed

    Some distance away
you can see, across paddies and woods,
    in this stunned glare of midday,
    six green shades like moods

    that betray the villes
we have been patrolling since first light,
    humping for the far foothills –
    as if in mad flight

    from the privation
of palm-leaf huts, wood hoes, small pieces
    of china, and eyes that shun
    our faceless faces.

    There are no young men:
they are hiding, Viet Cong, or dead.
    Only the old folk, children,
    and empty-breasted

    mothers still remain,
survivors among all their wreckage.
    Are they trying to retain
    some hold? Or to edge

    from a commitment,
patiently waiting out their desire?
    I don't know. Once arrogant,
    bringing aid, the fire

              of napalm, and lead,
I become one of their witnesses
         to history: this seedbed
             with its crevices

           sluicing through earth's crust;
this seedbed, like a dry pod shaken
      over a dead land, like lust
           without a woman.

Letter from a Ward

Commandos empty of your manhood, cease
Prowling over this unlit no-man's land
And leave me, if not consolation, peace.
    Go down among the Picts,

Spartans, and Roman Legionaries, hidden
In whirls of brackish vapors: a rowdy band
Boasting of bawdry and of war, wine-sodden,
    Bivouacked along the Styx.

Chaplain to Bishop

I bless them in the bush,
Knowing what they confront:
Not so much death and pain
As power and extreme want,
The need of will to push
Through jungle gorged with rain.

Like them, I have my duty.
I bring them sacraments;
Preach love of the enemy,
Christ on His cross, a sense
Of sacrificial beauty.
However, now I see

Here is no compromise,
Even, but dereliction
Or absolute defeat.
In chapel, their dull eyes
Mirror my heart's conviction.
I see my self-deceit.

POWs

Lieutenant Gilbert took us down the hill
This morning at first light, sweeping a ville
For sympathizers. I am guarding two:
A hunchbacked mama-san and her child, who
Squat, fingers quick, blindfolded, loosely bound.
It's odd, but neither makes the smallest sound,
Kneading this silence that I cannot fill.

Da Nang Nights
liberty song

The streets are dark and misty,
Until we near the strip
Where bar girls and weak whiskey
Burn the blistered lip.

In sudden light we choose
Lust by lust our bar;
And whatever else we lose,
We also lose the war.

Running in Vietnam

One hundred four degrees: the war's remote
As you dress right in the PT formation,
Although you know the gunny's threat by rote:

'The gooks are all around us!' Aberration?
A mad old lifer's deepest wishful thought?
Eighteen years, two wars, a police action:

He's seen it all, while you have merely fought
In *this* war, at *this* time. He orders, 'Left face!
Quick time, march!' Your every muscle taut,

You stomp in a jog step, finding a place
In keeping time, as mushrooms of dust fill
Your vision, even as they let him trace

The increased progress winding down the hill.
Six miles to the PX; then the return,
The last five miles a steep grade. Only will

Could push through corrugating heat to earn
Two lukewarm beers, trooper, you will not drink.
The duty tour drags on, and you will learn

The only quick time's running, though you sink
Without a second wind, whatever gunnies think.

Office of the Dead

Death's mostly distant here of late,
And random with the seediness
Of plain bad luck – nothing like Fate.
But the dead are neither more nor less:

Just dead. I check their metal tags
For eight hours, till my duty ceases,
Body-counting the body bags.
I do not have to count the pieces.

Sniper

They command, and I obey,
collecting my combat pay.
Peasant, soldier – it's all one
on this hill where, like passion
seeking an object, I wait
and, watching, I concentrate.
It's truth of a kind, this sense
of sighting down the long lens
at men who scurry to loss,
hung on my spider web cross.

First Watch

The land crawls like a distant ocean
Beneath the mist – there is no sky –
As leeches set the trails in motion.
Night closes. My poncho keeps me dry
Where, huddled on this ragged shelf,
I sit in darkness, sealed in self.

Short-Timer: Six and a Wakeup

Of bush-time memories, this lingers:
A mountain outpost with two fingers
Like a crab's pincers that hooked down,
South to a valley; an ash mound
And scorched earth starkly documented
The rage some grunt platoon once vented;
And just beyond, at the far edge
A long berm formed a kind of ledge
Below which ran a dirt-packed road
Equipped to handle any load.
Between the pincers, tangled brush
Grew to eight feet; and in it, lush
Green vines, heat, and humidity
Were dense as the South China Sea.

Souvenirs

Da Nang Air Terminal: slouching, small groups
Of shabby short-timers harass the troops
Just disembarked in-country, flaunting flags,
Belt buckles, carbines, gold teeth, and old rags
Of uniforms stripped from the enemy
Or the black market.
                        Everywhere I see
Cunning old salts mount guard on foreign gear
As if they'll need reminders they fought here.

Elegy for a Dead Friend

Mock night of black clouds seemingly withdrew
Into deep space; then our break ended too.

Was it the quickened beauty of that day
That made you careless as you forced your way

Beyond the hut's packed earth, through the hedgerows?
Was it that letter? Simply chance? Who knows?

You tripped a mine. Explosion and then scream –
Blast and echo – I heard them in a dream

Of foliage. Dirt fell. Smoke caught my eye
As it drifted across the china sky.

    First to reach you, I saw the uniform
Ragged, knee-length, but could not keep you warm

For all my curses, for all my first aid,
Feeling that I, not you, had been betrayed.

You lay there. I, who thought myself long hardened,
Learned fear extended beyond self-regard.

As if that mine was a mirror you confronted,
Face pressed to glass, no matter what I wanted,

You would not slip past, leaving me this loss,
Liking too much your sudden helplessness.

'The Lighter That Never Fails'

Like brambles twisted in a thicket, six huts,
Unmapped, lay squat in jungle on our flank.
We took fire. After mortars and a tank
Cleared the guerrillas, we swept, our rifle butts
At ready, through civilians left to us.
Rice caches and dead buddies – God's grim sign
To His Elect – prompted us when, on line,
We judged the sympathizers: righteous
With Zippos, torching their thatched homes, we built
Altars, then scattered ashes, scattered guilt.

Last Letter

We're haunting these same mountains yet again,
Tracking down phantoms, and my weariness
Soaks in like fear. It deadens even pain.

This afternoon, we found twelve carcasses
Around bomb craters. Though I choked on the smell
Of maggot-breeding flesh at first, I bless

Those bodies now, for they are flaunting hell;
Bless them, for they are shattered and awry;
Bless them, for I have heard the truth they tell:

'Come, friend, it is not difficult to die.'

Meditations after Battle

I. *Sunt lacrimae rerum ...*

And all around, the dead! So many dead!
So many ways to die it hurt the heart
To look and feel sun burning overhead.
We stacked the bodies on scorched grass, apart.

II *... et mentem mortalia tangunt*

Death was the context and the only fact.
Amidst the stench, I almost could believe
There was a world of light where, if souls lacked
Broken bodies awhile, they would retrieve
Them, mended, where no one need longer grieve.

Fieldcraft

At last, the senses sharpen. All around,
I listen closely. Under the dull sound
Of distant artillery and the shrieking planes
Diving with napalm; under the dry crack
Of automatic rifles; at the back
Of consciousness, almost, one sound remains:
Mud sucking at bare feet as they are going
Between the rice shoots. Nearly silent. Knowing.

A Letter from the World
March 1969

You'll never come in from your last patrol.
Down to six spades – your short-time calendar –
You count long rations left, each fighting hole,
Certain you know exactly where you are

When your reflections snap from dwindling days
To clean clothes, women, loafing, and cold beer.
And yet that reverie indulged betrays
The horrors you contain; and once back here,

As you'll discover, you must sleep at night,
Walking one more patrol; relearn, in bed,
Paddies, jungle, fear, till with the first light
You're oily with the rancor of the dead.

III

'Why not adjust? Forget this? ... '

Why not adjust? Forget this? Let it be?
Because it's truth. Because it's history.

De Bello

The troops deploy. Above, the stars
Wheel over mankind's little wars.
If there's a deity, it's Mars.

'Patrolling silently ... '

Patrolling silently,
He knows how men will die
In jungles. I am he.
He is not I.

Definition

The epigram is not artillery,
Blockbuster, napalm, mortar, rocketry;
But it is, rather, hunkered deep in mire,
The sniper-scoped guerrilla's small arms fire.

SOP

I learned what soldiers learn: neither a flag
Nor brassy phrases count much, under fire.
Men fight from pride, grief, fear of censure; mostly,
Though, it's closest buddies who evoke
Some kind of courage, if only hanging on.

Social Darwinism

Professionally aided,
The Privileged became,
Until the danger faded,
The weak and halt and lame.

For Part of a Generation

Worn out, the toaster, television, car
Are thrown out, junked, or traded for the new
Just as America abandoned you:
Conspicuous consumption, Asian war.

'Don't you know your poems are hurtful?'

Yes, ma'am. Like KA-BAR to the gut,
Well-tempered wit should thrust and cut
Before the victim knows what's what;
But sometimes, lest the point be missed,
I give the bloody blade a twist.

Grunt Fantasy

Another war and, swabbing tears with sleeves,
Over the coffin a rich mother grieves.

Epitaph for the Fallen at Camerone
after an inscription in Les Invalides

Fewer than sixty soldiers lie here, but they fought
An army till submerged in its immensity.
Though life deserted these French troops, honor did not
That 30th day of April, 1863.

Foxhole Theology

Of all the prayers enticed
    Under the gun,
I've never heard *Sweet Christ,*
    Thy will be done.

Martial 8.58

You wear an army surplus coat; it suits you,
    Until some passerby salutes you.

Reading the Op-Ed Page
I missed my generation's test.

Yuppie's nostalgic consonants and vowels
Prove that, though wanting guts, he still has bowels.

Incoming!
and the mist swirled ...

Ares once cloaked his heroes in such seeming mists
As now erupt around us on the battlefield
Where spouting shrapnel, mud and smoke cloak riflemen
Whose scattered bodies neither can be healed nor saved.

As Good as It Gets

A break from humping, bug juice zapping leeches,
Three sips of water, and pound cake and peaches.

'Tonight you bitch ... '

Tonight you bitch, under too many drinks,
'Fucked over! Got our asses kicked for dinks!'
I leave the obvious alone – in fact,
For wealthy children, to keep theirs intact.

After the War
for Dan Quayle et al.

It's tough to find, however hard one seeks,
Old khaki stripes among the yellow streaks.

Lessons of War

Hump extra rounds, frags, canteen, or long ration,
But always shitcan the imagination.

'Kentucky's Money Bonus'

> *Kentuckians who served in Vietnam ...*
> *are entitled to $25 for each month of service,*
> *with a maximum bonus of $300.*

Blood money, conscience cash adjusted
To time in-country and they're quit.
What makes me so goddamned disgusted:
Their offer? My accepting it?

Ambush

For thirteen months, death was familiar.
We knew its methods and the odds. Thus, war.
And yet, I never once saw dying eyes
That were not stunned or shattered by surprise.

MIAs

Ghostly, we are like disembodied sounds:
Voices afar, echoes diminishing.

A Little Elegy for Jimmy Stewart

I honor you for this: unlike John Wayne –
'America's embodiment?' Straight scoop:
Embodied the know-nothing or the dupe –
You knew first hand war's suffering and pain
And consequently never played a scene
Perverting combat on a movie screen.

Snapshot, RVN

I see us there, as we were then,
Sinewy, strong and very young
Lounging in pre-formation when
The camera snapped – and I am stung
Seeing such blasted innocence
That we have carried ever since.

'I swore I'd only be ... '

I swore I'd only be a three year cypher
But learn each sweaty midnight I'm a lifer.

Epitaph for a Patrol Leader

The medals did not signify –
No more than his suntan –
Nor the promotions; simply say,
'He never lost a man.'

IV

Coda

Republic of Vietnam Campaign Medal with Device

See 1960— but nothing follows;
And in that missing date a country's lost:
  Overrun, routed, and dissolved,
Unable, even, to document its ending.

But all the troops who rate that medal, ah,
For them their several dates are to be read,
  Or will be read, in cemeteries
As each man comes in from his last patrol.

[Note: the dash following 1960 must be pronounced]